COLORING BOOK

Mehregaan: **The Triumph of Liberty over Tyranny**

Dr. Khodadad (Khodi) Kaviani

Printed in the United States

ISBN-13: 978-0692895962
ISBN-10: 0692895965

جشن مهرگان بر همگان خجسته باد!

Merry Mehregaan to All!

ACKNOWLEDGEMENTS

Thank you, Soumen Sarkar, for turning my rough sketches into beautiful illustrations for this story.

I am also thankful to Michelle Rostami for page set up and consulting.

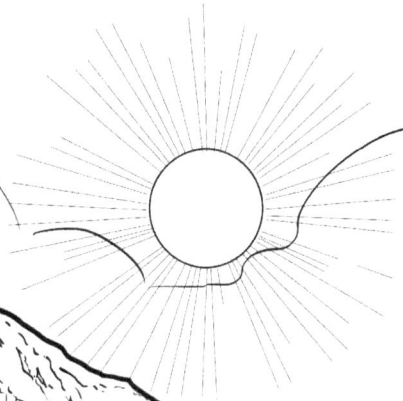

گر ایدونکه دانید من کردم این
مرا خواند باید جهان آفرین

I did it all, knows every arbitrator!
Indeed, I am the Great Creator!

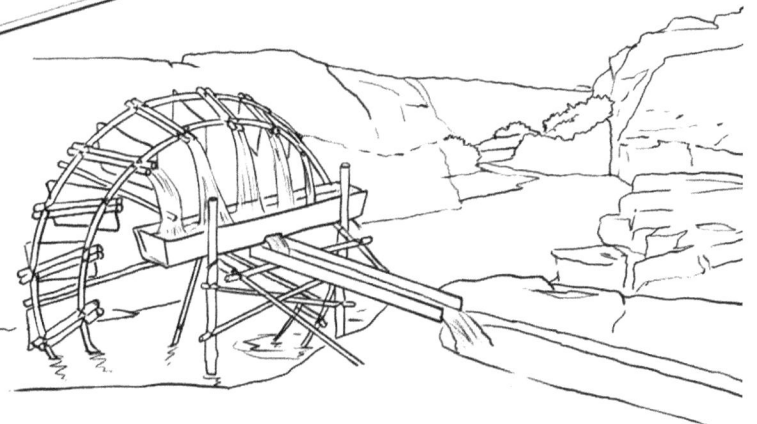

خور و خواب و آرامتان از من است همان پوشش و کامتان از من است
Because of me, you have food, sleep, and security,
Even your clothes and dreams of happy futurity!

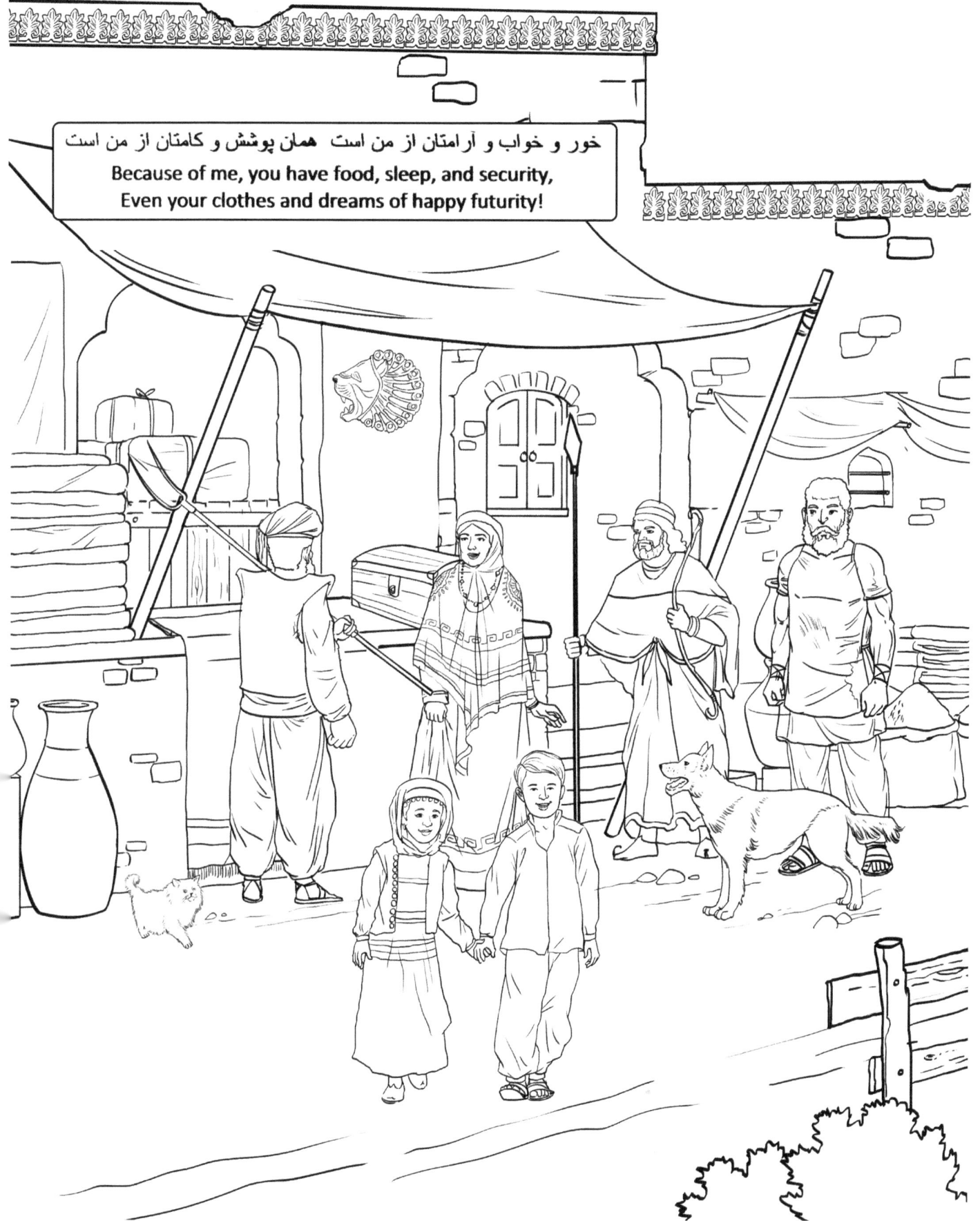

از آن پس برآمد ز ایران خروش پدید آمد از هر سویی جنگ و جوش
After that, from Iran came voices of unrest,
Popping everywhere war and protest.

فراوان سخن گفت زیبا و نغز   جوان را ز دانش تهی بود مغز

Said a lot of nice words eloquently,
Unexperienced youth fooled evidently!

سواران ایران **همه شاه جوی** نهادند یکسر به ضحاک روی
Iranian riders wanting a king,
Headed for Zah-haak, betting everything

هنر خوار شد جادویی ارجمند   نهان راستی آشکارا گزند
Virtue lost its place, and trickery was prized,
Truth went into hiding, and corruption disguised!

شده بر بدی دست دیوان دراز   ز نیکی نبودی سخن جز به راز
Sleazy hand stretched conveniently,
No sound of goodness, except secretly!

MEET AND GREET YOUR KING

که بر من زمانه کی آید بسر
کرا باشد این تاج و تخت و کمر

When will my time end, according to hand dealt,
Who will have this crown, throne and lovely belt?

نشان فریدون بگرد جهان   همی باز جست آشکار و نهان
Looked for signs of Fereidoon all over the world,
Searched where he could see, even hidden world.

ندارم همی دشمن خرد خوار   بترسم همی از بد روزگار
I don't underestimate small enemies,
I am scared of bad fate adversaries!

MEET AND GREET YOUR KING

بده داد من کامدستم دوان   همی نالم از تو برنج روان
I have ran here to get justice,
My soul is hurt of your injustice!

If seven countries have you as their king,
Why we receive your never-ending sting?!

اگر هفت کشور به شاهی تراست
چرا رنج و سختی همی بهر ماست

همی برخروشید و فریاد خواند
جهان را سراسر سوی داد خواند

Rise up! declared in a shouting voice,
World needs justice, a real true choice!

از آن چرم کاهنگران پشت پای   بپوشند هنگام زخم درای
همان کاوه آن بر سر نیزه کرد همانگه ز بازار برخاست گرد

From that leather apron metalsmiths wear,
When forging metals, fire in the air,
Kaaveh put it atop a long spear,
People joining him eager with cheer!

We want freedom!

Justice now!

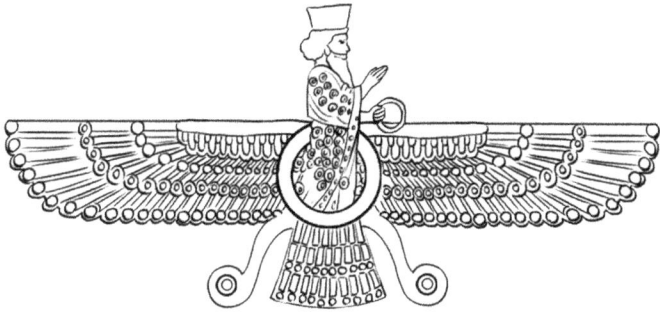

فروهشت از او زرد و سرخ و بنفش
همی خواندش کاویانی درفش
Hanging from it, yellow, red, purple,
Kaviani Flag, symbol eternal!

که یزدان پاک از میان گروه   برانگیخت ما را ز البرز کوه
بدان تا جهان از بد اژدها   بفرمان و گرز من آید رها
The Holy Creator chose us for certain,
To lead the charge from Alborz Mountain,
Know the world will get rid of this dragon monster,
With my order, and grace of my mace! No more mobster!

PERSIAN GULF

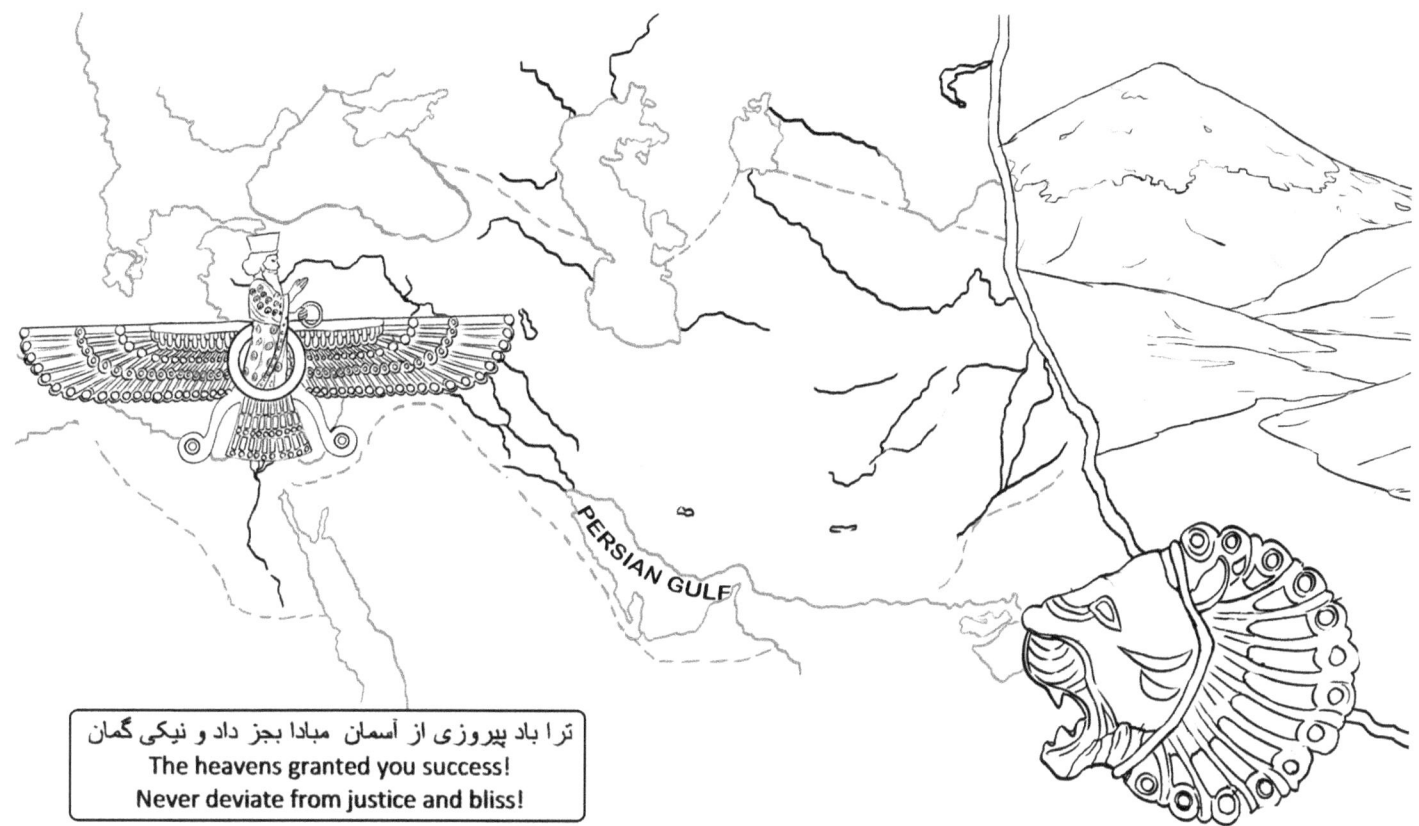

ترا باد پیروزی از آسمان مبادا بجز داد و نیکی گمان
The heavens granted you success!
Never deviate from justice and bliss!

بروز خجسته سر مهر ماه   بسر بر نهاد آن کیانی کلاه
دل از داوری ها بپرداختند   بآیین یکی جشن نو ساختند
پرستیدن مهرگان دین اوست   تن آسانی و خوردن آیین اوست

On this blessed day in month of Mehr,
Wore the Kiani Crown, he was the heir.
Declared truce, ended all conflicts,
Made a new holiday, for people to mix.
Worshipping Mehr is his belief,
Resting and eating, peaceful motif.

"I created Mehr to be worthy of praise and prayer.
Whoever lies to Mehr, breaks promises and is unfaithful,
destroys the country and kills the truth.
O holy one [Zoroaster], you must not break your promise,
no matter with a Mazdayasnaa or with an evil doer,
because once you have concluded an agreement with whomever,
then that commitment is true and worthy of respect."
Mehr Yasht.

16 Mehr	17 Soroosh	18 Rashn	19 Farvardeen	20 Verahraam	21 Raam

که جاوید بادا چنین روزگار
برومند بادا چنین شهریار
May such days last forever!
Cheers for this king, stronger ever!